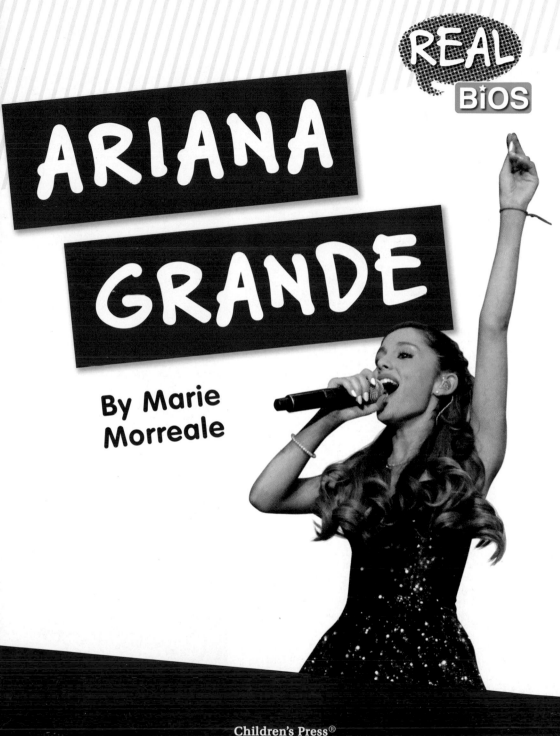

ARIANA GRANDE

By Marie Morreale

Children's Press®
An Imprint of Scholastic Inc.
New York   Toronto   London   Auckland   Sydney
Mexico City   New Delhi   Hong Kong
Danbury, Connecticut

Photographs ©: Alamy Images/Pictorial Press Ltd.: 40 top; AP Images: 12 (Alex J. Berliner/ABImages), 14, 24 top, 37 (Charles Sykes/Invision), 33 (Frank Micelotta/Invision), 2, 3 (John Shearer/Invision), 13 bottom (Julio Cortez), 18 top (Lisa Rose, Nickelodeon), 23 bottom left (Republic Records), 44 (Scott Gries/Invision); Dreamstime: 23 bottom right, 40 (Featureflash), 15 bottom right (Ingvar Bjork); Getty Images: 34 (Amy Sussman), 25 (Bobby Bank), 16, 23 top (Bruce Glikas), 22 bottom left (Chris McKay), 20 bottom (Earl Gibson III), 22 bottom right (JB Lacroix), 28 (Jeff Kravitz), 7 left, 43 bottom right (Jim Spellman), 20 top (Kevin Mazur), 24 bottom (Kevin Winter), 32 (Kevork Djansezian), 9 (Larry Busacca), 26 (Michael Stewart), back cover (Michael Tran), 30 (NBC), 38 top (Ray Tamarra), cover (Rich Polk/AMA2013), 38 center (Taylor Hill); iStockphoto/Antagain: 37; Newscom: 27, 42 (BSA/ZOJ WENN Photos), 1, 35 (Derek Storm/Splash News), 7 right, 10 (infusny-236/Walter McBride/INFphoto.com), 15 center left (St Petersburg Times/Zumapress); REX USA : 18 bottom, 19 (Henry Lamb/BEImages), 31 (Masatoshi Okauchi), 6, 7 background (Veda Jo Jenkins); Shutterstock, Inc.: 15 top (Annette Shaff), 13 top center (chrupka), 13 top right (endeavor), 43 top right (Featureflash), 38 bottom, 42 right, 43 top left (Helga Esteb), 39 bottom (Jaguar PS), 13 top left (Kerstin Schoene), 21, 39 top (s_bukley); StarTraksPhoto: 8, 22 top, 41 top (Albert Michael), 4, 5 (Michael Simon); Superstock, Inc./M.G.M./Album: 43 bottom left; Thinkstock: 36 (Ira Bachinskaya), 15 bottom left (Jaroslav Filsh), 41 bottom (lirtlon), 15 center bottom (Mariusz Blach), 15 center right (Ton van de Laar), 13 center (Wavebreakmedia Ltd.).

Library of Congress Cataloging-in-Publication Data
Morreale, Marie.
  Ariana Grande / by Marie Morreale.
    pages cm. — (Real bios)
  Includes bibliographical references and index.
  ISBN 978-0-531-21197-7 (lib. bdg. : alk. paper) —
  ISBN 978-0-531-21272-1 (pbk. : alk. paper)
  1. Grande, Ariana—Juvenile literature. 2. Singers—United States—Biography—Juvenile literature. I. Title.
  ML3930.G724M67 2014
  782.42164092—dc23 [B]   2014004442

© 2015 Scholastic Inc.

All rights reserved. Published in 2015 by Children's Press, an imprint of Scholastic Inc.
Printed in the United States of America 113

SCHOLASTIC, CHILDREN'S PRESS, and associated logos are trademarks and/or registered trademarks of Scholastic Inc.

1 2 3 4 5 6 7 8 9 10 R 24 23 22 21 20 19 18 17 16 15

Ariana got a standing ovation at the 2013 American Music Awards. She sang "Tattooed Heart."

MEET ARIANA!

Ariana Grande . . . It seems you can't pick up a magazine or check the latest social media buzz on Twitter, Facebook, Instagram, YouTube, or Flickr without seeing updates about the costar of Nickelodeon's *Sam & Cat.* You can't flip a TV channel or radio station without seeing her sparkling face or hearing her four-**octave** voice soaring over the airwaves. Her hit album *Yours Truly* spawned three smash singles. She's won multiple awards, and she's traveled all over the globe winning new fans—called Arianators—everywhere.

   The 21-year-old actress/singer is a genuine superstar. Her voice has been compared to such musical divas as Mariah Carey, Whitney Houston, and Christina Aguilera—but that's just chatter. Ariana is Ariana. Read on and you will agree.

CONTENTS

Ariana poses for a selfie
with a true-blue Arianator!

ARIANA'S JOURNEY

FROM COAST TO COAST

SHE WAS BORN IN FLORIDA AND BECAME A STAR IN CALIFORNIA

Ariana Grande always knew she wanted to perform. Even as a little girl in her hometown of Boca Raton, Florida, she loved to entertain her family: parents Joan Grande and Edward Butera and older half brother, Frankie. She sparkled when friends and family would visit, and she recalls doing her original song-and-dance routines for them. "I know it sounds silly, but I started singing when I was two," Ariana told *J-14* magazine. "The first song I ever sang out loud was an *NSYNC song. I remember I was in the car with my mommy and she was like, 'Is that you? Can you do that again?'"

Not only did Ariana do it again, but she kept getting better and better. At just eight years old, she made her

Ariana's Christmas gift to Florida fans— she performed at the Y100 Jingle Ball.

Ariana appeared in the Broadway musical *13* in 2008.

"THERE WOULD BE A LOT OF MUSIC IN MY WORLD!"

Ariana spends a fun day of shopping and laughing with her older brother, Frankie.

first live TV appearance when she sang the national anthem at a Florida Panthers hockey game. That was the first big step to becoming the star she is today. "I knew that I wanted to be a performer since I was basically born," Ariana told Scholastic magazines. "I was always running around the house in costume and makeup. I was a different character every single day. I started doing community theater when I was eight."

Frankie, who was getting established as a singer/actor about that time, also encouraged her. Ariana followed in her big bro's footsteps and started making the audition rounds. The funny thing is that it wasn't a winning audition that convinced Ariana she was on the right career road. It was actually a **karaoke** performance she did while on a cruise with her family. She sang the theme from the movie *Titanic*, "My Heart Will Go On." Eight-year-old Ariana wasn't singing to just *any* audience. Oh no! Much to her surprise and delight, legendary singer Gloria Estefan was there. That alone would have been a story to share with her friends at home, but the magic didn't stop there. "Someone came over and said, 'Can we speak to your daughter?'" Ariana told crushable.com. "It was Gloria Estefan, and she says, 'Honey I just wanted to let you know that you have so much more than I did at your age. You

Legendary singer Gloria Estefan was an early fan of Ariana.

Just Ariana
"I try to just sing how I sing."

Broadway
Baby!
Starring in *13* was
just the first step
for Ariana's rise
to fame!

have to keep going because you were meant to do this.' She kind of inspired me and I've always loved performing, so that's kind of how I started."

Ariana soon won roles in local family theater productions in South Florida. "My first role was Annie [in *Annie*], and I remember loving the music but wanting to play Miss Hannigan," she laughingly told WZRA TV. "I was eight! After a few years of doing community theater and school plays, I started auditioning for Broadway and I got cast in *13*, which is where I began my professional career."

Ariana and fellow cast members of *13* pose for the camera.

ALL IN ARIANA'S FAMILY

*NSYNC songs, the national anthem, a karaoke version of "My Heart Will Go On," and *Annie's* "Tomorrow"—that's how Ariana started her journey to stardom. At the same time, the young Floridian had a personal life. When *Complex* magazine asked Ariana about her childhood, she answered, "My family was the **stereotypical** poker-playing, loud, friendly, food-shoving, loving Italian family. . . . My *nonna* [grandmother] is the best cook in the world. We had Sunday sauce—the best marinara sauce ever."

GIRL MEETS WORLD

Of course, Ariana has never pretended that her whole life was perfect. As a matter of fact, just when she was starting to follow her dream of performing, things were crumbling at home. "My parents got divorced when I was eight years old, and it was very hard for me," she told *Twist* magazine. "I lost my appetite completely. I couldn't eat, couldn't sleep, couldn't think . . . I couldn't take the stress of my parents getting divorced. . . . It was so upsetting, because I wanted to be together."

Things eventually settled down for Ariana and her family, but she still faced problems balancing her personal life

Yum-Yum
"A mango is like God thinking, 'I'm having a great day today!' He was like, 'You know, I like these people on earth!'"

and professional life. "I went right from middle school, like everyday school, to Broadway," she told neonlimelight.com. "That was a really crazy transition to make because it was so much hard work. I was like, 'Yay, no more school!' Then I was like, 'Oh my! I have to kill myself every day dancing for more than twelve hours and sit on my couch every day with Icy Hot and Tiger Balm and the whole house smelling like menthol and waiting for my muscle pain to go away.'"

In the end, Ariana was the first to admit that it was all worth it. Today, she says she

funfact:
Ariana has more than **15 million** Twitter followers!

FULL NAME Ariana Joan Grande-Butera

NICKNAMES Ari and Riri

BIRTHDAY June 26, 1993

ASTROLOGICAL SIGN Cancer

BIRTHPLACE Boca Raton, Florida

PARENTS Joan Grande and Edward Butera

HAIR COLOR Natural brown but dyed velvet red

EYE COLOR Brown

SIBLING Older half brother Frankie Butera

HERITAGE Italian

PETS Dogs named Coco and Toulouse

MIDDLE SCHOOL Pine Crest Middle School in Boca Raton

HIGH SCHOOL North Broward Preparatory School

MUSICAL INFLUENCES Mariah Carey, India.Arie, Whitney Houston

FIRST ROLE IN A MUSICAL Ariana played the lead role (Annie) in Annie at a South Florida community theater

PRIZED POSSESSION Her smartphone

CELEBRITY CRUSHES Justin Timberlake, Leonardo DiCaprio, Chris Pine

CURRENT MUSICAL CRUSH Bruno Mars

GUILTY PLEASURE Pop-Tarts

THROAT SOOTHERS Grether's Pastilles

DREAM SUPERPOWER To fly

HOBBY Photography

FASHION ICONS Marilyn Monroe, Audrey Hepburn

SECOND LANGUAGE Spanish

DREAM ROLE Elphaba in Wicked

FANS' NICKNAME Arianators

Thrills and Chills

"I love scary movies. I love dinosaurs, science, aliens, ghosts!"

13

has a great relationship with both her mom and dad. "Finally, after many years, [it's gotten] to the point where I'm OK with them being apart," she told *Twist*. As for her work life, Ariana summed it up to neonlimelight.com when she said, "It's a lot of hard work and it's a lot of adjusting, but I'm learning so much, so I'm happy."

You can believe Ariana when she says she is happy. But she has never forgotten where she comes from. She told the Miami Herald, "I think I've finally found what I'm meant to be doing. I hope my Florida fans will be proud of me."

"I HAVE MY OWN GARDEN IN MY BACKYARD. I HARVESTED JALAPEÑOS FROM MY GARDEN FOR THE FIRST TIME THE OTHER DAY."

PASTIMES Shopping, playing video games, and reading comic books

RELAXATION Listening to music

SPORT Swimming

BOOKS The Lord of the Rings and the Harry Potter series

SINGERS Katy Perry, Mariah Carey, Imogen Heap, Christina Aguilera, Celine Dion, Michael Jackson

BAND Bon Jovi

SONG FROM *YOURS TRULY* "Honeymoon Avenue"

ACTRESS Jennifer Garner

COLORS Periwinkle and coral

SNACK Fruit—especially strawberries, watermelon, mangoes, pears, and grapes

FOOD Sushi

DINNER Salmon

CANDIES Smarties and Razzles

CEREAL Cocoa Puffs

YOGURT Raspberry Greek yogurt

ICE CREAM Chocolate

TOPPING Rainbow sprinkles

COOKIES Parisian macarons

DRINK Coconut water

SPICE Garlic

BOCA RATON RESTAURANT Stir Crazy, an Asian grill

FASHION DESIGNER Chanel

SOCIAL MEDIA Twitter and Instagram **twitter**

DISNEY PRINCESS Sleeping Beauty's Aurora

MOVIE Breakfast at Tiffany's

NICKELODEON SERIES iCarly

Ariana can't believe she is a regular on the pages of the top teen magazines!

"I'M SO HAPPY THAT I'M GOING AFTER MY DREAMS."

LIFE IS GRANDE!

WATCH OUT—ARIANA HAS JUST STARTED!

At age 15, Ariana became a bright light on Broadway in the musical *13*. But it wasn't until she made her way to Nickelodeon that people started taking notice. She first made a guest appearance on *iCarly*. That was when her TV character, Cat Valentine, was introduced. Ariana/Cat soon moved on to the sitcom *Victorious* and its 2013 spin-off series, *Sam & Cat*.

FROM STAGE TO SCREEN

On each step up the ladder of success, Ariana was learning and listening. She wanted to know everything about a career in show business. She knew that was what she wanted to do forever. Comparing Broadway to TV, Ariana told crushable.com, "Both kinds of performances are amazing.

Wise Words

Ariana's grandfather told her, "May you live as long as you want to and laugh as long as you live."

Laverne and Shirley legends Penny Marshall and Cindy Williams guest star with Jennette McCurdy and Ariana on Sam & Cat.

Broadway is amazing because you're performing for such an intimate group of people. You're living in the moment and whatever happens happens, and you go on. You can't say cut and redo it—you have to be on the whole time. It's for a small group of people and you're feeding off their energy. When you're filming, it's also really awesome because an audience of, like, a million people [is] going to see it. And you have to stay there the whole day and

Ariana's Timeline

Follow Her Journey

JUNE 26, 1993
Ariana is born in Boca Raton, Florida.

2008
Ariana wins the National Youth Theatre Association Award for Best Actress for 13.

you get up really early and go into hair and makeup at the crack of dawn. It's really fun, both ways."

Victorious was a big break for Ariana, but *Sam & Cat* turned out to be an even bigger gift. Not only was she leaping from one hit sitcom to another, but also her costar, Jennette McCurdy, was one of her besties. They first performed together when Nickelodeon did a crossover episode between *iCarly* and *Victorious* called "iParty with Victorious."

Ariana clicked right away with Jennette, a regular on *iCarly*. The two friends also shared credits in the Nickelodeon TV movie, *Swindle*. When they were told they were going to star together in *Sam & Cat*, they were beyond happy! The funny thing is that although both Ariana and Jennette are singers, Nickelodeon decided that the series wasn't going to have a musical element.

"I SURROUND MYSELF WITH THE PEOPLE I LOVE."

MARCH 27, 2010
Nickelodeon's sitcom *Victorious* debuts with Ariana playing the role of Cat.

2011
Ariana voices the character Princess Diaspro in the animated TV series *Winx Club: Enchantix*.

DECEMBER 12, 2011
Ariana releases her first single, "Put Your Hearts Up."

Katy Perry and Ariana backstage at the 2013 MTV Europe Music Awards

That was okay with Ariana. It gave her more time to work on her own music. Even with all of her acting success, Ariana never gave up her dream of working on her debut album, which was originally going to be called *Daydreamin'*. She worked in her home studio using Apple's GarageBand software. She trained with voice coach Eric Vetro, who has also worked with Katy

DECEMBER 2012
Ariana stars with Neil Patrick Harris in a stage production of *A Snow White Christmas* at the Pasadena Playhouse.

MARCH 25, 2013
"The Way" debuts on *On Air with Ryan Seacrest.*

MARCH 28, 2013
The music video for "The Way" is released.

APRIL 5, 2013
"The Way" becomes Ariana's first *Billboard* Hot 100 top 10 hit.

JUNE 8, 2013
Ariana stars as Cat in the *Victorious* spinoff *Sam & Cat.*

Perry. "I met Katy through him," Ariana enthused to JustJared Jr.com. "She's such a sweet woman. I love her—she's one of my inspirations; I look up to her."

MAKING MUSIC MAGIC

Ariana loved every minute of working on her album—both on her own and when she signed with Republic Records. Republic connected her with legendary singer/songwriter and producer Kenneth "Babyface" Edmonds. The highlight of her day was when she could hit the recording studio. "If I could, I would not do anything else," Ariana told *Elle* magazine. "I'd just be in the studio for my whole life. I would never go to parties, events, and red carpets. I would rather just be in the studio for the whole time. I don't even care. Nobody has to know

Instagram Manners
"Not too many selfies. Space them out—you have to wait a few days in between selfies."

JUNE 19, 2013
"The Way" is certified platinum after it sells more than 1 million copies.

JULY 1, 2013
Ariana wins Best Newcomer at the *Billboard* Mid-Year Music Awards.

JULY 22, 2013
The single "Baby I" is released.

AUGUST 7, 8, AND 10, 2013
Ariana opens for Justin Bieber on his Believe tour.

Karaoke Candy

"[I love] 'Lady Marmalade'—that's always a fun one."

what I look like. I just want to make music."

Ariana's dedication paid off. When she released "The Way," the first single from her then upcoming album, *Yours Truly*, she totally blew up! When Ariana first heard "The Way," she knew it was something special. She asked her good friend Mac Miller to work with her on it, and he said yes! "I went over to his house," she told Yahoo.com. "I **engineered** the session. I recorded him rapping, while I was simultaneously baking cookies for him and that was that."

AUGUST 13, 2013
Ariana begins her first **headlining** tour, called Listening Sessions.

AUGUST 24, 2013
Ariana stars in Nickelodeon's TV movie *Swindle*.

AUGUST 25, 2013
Ariana makes her MTV Video Music Awards debut— she sings "Baby I" and "The Way" on the preshow.

With the release of *Yours Truly*, Ariana went to the top of the music charts. And, as much as she believed in her album, Ariana was surprised at the musical explosion she caused. "I never realized until now how many more people I could reach with music," she told *Billboard* magazine. "I've been so lucky to be on television for such a long time and to make kids and their families so happy, but this is something different."

In the summer of 2013, Ariana was extremely busy. Not only was she filming *Sam & Cat*, but she also had to prepare to open for the last three concerts of

Ariana debuts her first album, *Yours Truly*, in August 2013.

AUGUST 30, 2013
Ariana's debut album, *Yours Truly*, is released.

SEPTEMBER 11, 2013
Yours Truly debuts at number one on the *Billboard* 200 chart.

OCTOBER 1, 2013
Ariana and singer Mika perform on *Dancing with the Stars*—they sing Mika's "Popular Song."

Justin Bieber's Believe tour. Shortly after that, Ariana launched her own nine-city headlining tour, Listening Sessions. Before she jumped in for those tours, Ariana told MTV News, "I'm training my voice to get used to singing every day because I took a long break from singing every single day because I was filming [*Sam & Cat*]. . . . Lots of vocal rest, lots of tea, lots of getting ready."

Kiss Kiss! Ariana loves meeting and greeting her fans!

NOVEMBER 6, 2013
Ariana announces on Twitter that she will release a Christmas song each week starting on November 19.

NOVEMBER 23, 2013
Ariana wins New Artist of the Year at the American Music Awards and performs "Tattooed Heart" at the ceremony.

NOVEMBER 28, 2013
Ariana performs "Last Christmas" with Dora the Explorer in Macy's Thanksgiving Day Parade.

Ariana needed the vocal work because after *Yours Truly* was released in late August 2013, she was singing and interviewing nonstop. The album debuted at number one on the Billboard 200 chart, which means it was a major success right away! In an interview with MTV News, Ariana explained why she is so proud of *Yours Truly*. "People got to know me first as an actress, but my mom said I'm a singer who acts on the side, but now they are gonna get to know Ariana the little brunette girl from Boca who loves music more than anything. And that's very exciting to me and it's very relatable."

Unfortunately, Ariana may have done a little too much talking after *Yours Truly* was released. Only days after the album hit stores, Ariana had to stop talking and singing. Doctors' orders! She had strained her vocal cords. Her doctors said she had to have complete vocal rest for a week.

> "I GREW UP WRITING SONGS IN MY ROOM ON GARAGEBAND."

DECEMBER 4, 2013
Ariana performs at the Rockefeller Center tree-lighting ceremony.

JANUARY 8, 2014
Ariana wins Favorite Breakout Artist at the 2014 People's Choice Awards.

MARCH 29, 2014
Ariana wins Favorite TV Actress at Nickelodeon's 2014 Kids' Choice Awards.

JULY 17, 2014
After one year as a series, *Sam & Cat* aired its final episode.

AUGUST 25, 2014
Ariana released her second album, *My Everything*.

"For those of u asking about my voice I screamed too much at my party totally irresponsible but it's better now, thanks for the well wishes," she tweeted to her fans.

Ariana followed her doctor's orders, and she was back in vocal shape quickly. This was a lucky break, because she had a breathtaking schedule for the rest of the year. From making an appearance on *Dancing with the Stars* to winning Best New Artist at the 2013 American Music Awards to singing "Last Christmas" while riding a float in the Macy's Thanksgiving Day Parade, Ariana was racking up those frequent-flier miles!

Ariana didn't get a break after the whirlwind of the holidays. She had to prepare for the release of her second album in 2014. Back in September 2013, she told Yahoo.com, "I've

Happy Thanksgiving from Ariana, Dora the Explorer, and Macy's!

come up with a few, two songs already, that I want on it. It's an album that I want to do a little bit different. I don't want it to sound like an extension of *Yours Truly*. I want it to sound like an evolution. I want to explore more sounds and experiment a little."

In the early spring of 2014, Ariana was so excited about the upcoming release of her sophomore album that she tweeted out an alert to her fans. "Great meeting tonight :) very excited for these next few months & for you all to hear some new music and by some I mean a lot."

On April 27, 2014, Ariana released her first single, "Problem," from her new album *My Everything*—which was released on August 25, 2014. And although *Sam & Cat* was cancelled in July 2014, Ariana is going to be very busy for a long time to come.

Ariana and mom, Joan, shop till they drop at the fabulous Los Angeles store, Chanel Boutique.

Shop, Shop, Shop

"Ariana loves . . . getting out 10,000 lip glosses or body sprays," says BFF Jennette McCurdy. "[She smells like] some sort of vanilla cupcake!"

Ariana greets fans at the 2013 MTV Europe Music Awards in Amsterdam.

UP CLOSE WITH
ARIANA

AMERICA'S SWEETHEART ANSWERS YOUR QUESTIONS

The minute Ariana enters a room, the cameras start flashing and the questions start flying. Reporters and fans alike want to know everything about her. The actress/singer has gotten used to all the attention, but she would rather talk one-on-one with a fan than hold a major press conference. No glitz, no glamour, just the facts. That's Ariana's first choice. Here are her answers to some of her fans' most asked questions.

On her dream house . . . "[It would be] a house that was big enough to have all my family in. I'd move everyone in together. I don't like the idea of being alone. I always have to have a big group of people about, like friends or family. I'd like to live with people who are fun, but at the same time chilled—not too crazy. To share a place with somebody, you have to be able to respect their space and chill when they need to."

On her food choices . . .

"I lost a bit of weight last year. It's 'cause I stopped eating junk food and started making healthy choices. I was happy with the way I was before and I'm still happy now, just healthier! But the lifestyle change isn't about being skinnier."

On advice for kids who want to act . . . "I would say to not be discouraged by any of the bad feedback you may get from casting directors or anyone. There are such silly reasons why you won't get cast for roles. I mean, if you audition for something and don't get the part, the worst thing you could do is take it personally or give up on yourself."

On what she'd choose to do for the rest of her life—singing or acting . . . "Singing, times a million!"

On dyeing her hair "red velvet" for *Victorious* and *Sam & Cat* . . . "I am really thankful that Dan Schneider, our executive producer, decided to have me dye my hair this color because I get to be different. I love being different. I do get a lot of attention for it as well. I think the color excites people, and whether they see it on TV or in person they are drawn to it, regardless of if they know me or not."

On her perfect day . . . "My perfect day would be if I could mix my LA life with my NYC life. I would start my day on the set . . . with my friends there, Dan [Schneider], the cast, the amazing writers, the incredible producers, and everyone! And then I would go see a Broadway show, and then I would go sing at Birdland, have sushi with my family, and then I would go home and play Wii with [friends]."

Ariana arrives at Japan's Narita International Airport to promote her new album.

On comparing Cat with herself . . . "I would never feel comfortable playing Cat with any other color hair than red, but I also feel most comfortable being myself with brown hair. . . . I'm really nothing like my character—we're both girly, but that's about it. I'm very quiet; I don't like to go out and party. So I get to be myself when I have brown hair and then I get to be Cat when I have red hair! It's like a *Hannah Montana* life."

Ariana and singer Miguel present an award at the 2014 Grammy Awards.

Ariana wows the audience at the 2013 MTV Video Music Awards.

On her songwriting routine . . . "I started writing songs when I was probably 12, but the thing about me writing songs is I can't sit down and try to write a song. I can sit down and try to write a song, but most of my songs that are my favorites that I've written literally just pop into my head. I don't know how it happens. I'm just like, 'Whoa! Oh my gosh, I have to write this down right now.' I'll be like, 'Mom give me your iPhone, I have to record this right now, hold on.' In the grocery store, I go into the milk aisle where no one is and I'm singing in the corner. It's cool."

On her favorite books . . . "Any Harry Potter book! I am obsessed with the Harry Potter books. They're genius. . . . I'm the biggest Harry Potter geek ever. When I was in school, we had to read *The Giver* as an assignment, and I actually really liked it!"

Family fun! Ariana and brother Frankie attend the Broadway in South Africa Concert.

On her charity, Broadway in South Africa . . .

"My brother is one of the cofounders, and we're sponsored by Keep a Child Alive, so our motto is they keep them alive and we give them life. We try to go [to South Africa] every January. . . . We take a few days and go to . . . teach the kids about music and dance and improv and theater and art. And I covered "ABC" by Michael Jackson. We taught them a dance to that, so it was really, really fun. . . . I think I learned just as much from them as I taught them."

On the first day at a new school . . .

"That's my favorite thing. First day of school, especially at a new school. You get to totally choose who you are with your friends. You get to be the class clown or you can be the girl next door, you can be quiet, a "mathlete." That's when you get to make your impression on your friends. . . . I was always outgoing. I was never a class clown. I was never too crazy, but I loved making friends and making jokes. I kind of stood up to people who were being bullies. . . . They would be bullying somebody, and I would turn it into a complete joke. I don't know how I did it, but everybody just started laughing and everyone was like, 'That's so stupid, why would anyone do that?'"

On if she could be a member of any band . . .

"The Beatles. They're classic. Of course, the Beatles."

Ariana sings her heart out during a 2013 concert!

ARIANA ON FASHION, FITNESS, FUN, AND MORE!

HERE'S A SCRAPBOOK OF EVERYTHING ARIANA GRANDE! GET A PEEK AT THE REAL ARIANA . . . AND MAYBE A GIGGLE, TOO!

funfact: Ariana is allergic to cats, shellfish, and bananas.

MOST EMBARRASSING MOMENT

"I was in the middle of performing in a play one time, and was dancing on stage in front of so many people, when my shoe fell off into the audience," Ariana recalled. "Luckily it landed in my best friend's lap—she quickly pushed it back to me on stage. I grabbed it and took it with me when I walked off, but it was still totally embarrassing."

STAR CHATTER

Mac Miller (collaborator on "The Way"):
"[Ariana] is a very, very talented singer, like she can sing incredibly. And that's awesome and she's a great person. She's one of the . . . nicest people I've ever met in my life."

Kelly Clarkson (after seeing Ariana on *The Ellen DeGeneres Show*):
"Okay, who the heck is this girl & where did she come from?! Someone just sent me this & wow she is killer & only 19!"

Demi Lovato:
"[Ariana] has vocals that are just unbelievable, and I have so much respect for her because she is a true singer. She's someone that I feel like is going to have a long career because of her voice, and I think she's going to be a huge name. She's gonna be great."

ABOUT ARIANA

Avan Jogia, *Victorious* costar:
"I always thought [Ariana] was going to be a big deal. She has a great voice and she's dedicated. She's who she wants to be . . . she wanted it."

Ariana's manager, Scooter Braun:
"She reminds me of both Mariah [Carey] and Christina [Aguilera]. Christina was this young, petite girl with this gigantic voice and Ariana has the same thing. And her tone and her range remind me of Mariah . . ."

Ariana's *13* and *Victorious* costar Elizabeth Gillies:
"[*Victorious* was] our fourth job together . . . we shared a dressing room for *13* and we lived together last year. It's been a crazy journey for us, knowing each other and knowing where we started and where we are now, it's amazing to see the transformation."

MUSICAL ROLE MODELS

Ariana loves **Imogen Heap** and says, "I'm absolutely her number one fan. I appreciate her musicality so much. Her brain is musical heaven."

Ariana's flashback inspiration is singer/actress **Judy Garland.** "I grew up watching videos of her concerts and movies," Ariana recalled. "I love how she tells a story when she sings. It was just about her voice and the words she was singing—no strings attached or silly hair or costumes, just a woman singing her heart out."

India.Arie is definitely on Ariana's iPod! "Her voice is heaven," Ariana says. "It's so soothing, and her lyrics are so healing and delicious. Her music makes me feel like everything is going to be okay."

Whitney Houston was very important to Ariana. "Whitney holds such a special place in my heart," Ariana said. "She inspired me to start singing as a little girl. . . . Her riffs are so precise and I love her tone. She's my inspiration."

Brandy wraps up Ariana's list. "I'm obsessed with the sweetness of her voice and I love her songs," Ariana admits. "Her riffs are also incredibly on point. Nothing excites me more than an extraordinarily precise run."

DANCE!
ARIANA-STYLE
WORKOUT!

FITNESS BUFF

GYM MACHINE
Elliptical

WORKOUT MUSIC
Nicki Minaj & Bruno Mars

CARDIO WORKOUT:
Dancing

HEALTHY DRINK:
Coconut water

HEALTHY SNACK:
Almonds and cashews

OUTDOOR EXERCISE
Jogging

HEALTH ADVICE
"Eat healthy, drink lots of water, meditate."

FASHIONISTA

PERSONAL STYLE

"Girly and classic—it's inspired by the 1950s, my favorite era for music and fashion. . . . I like to mix it up. It's a cross between classic, Audrey Hepburn inspired, old school, ladylike style, and boho chic, hippie, Aztec, cuddly style."

STYLE ADVICE

"You don't have to wear what's trendy to feel your prettiest."

MUST-HAVES

Big floppy hats, poofy skirts, maxi dresses, hair bows, polka dots, **pink anything**.

OOPS!

Kesha once told Ariana (who was wearing a pink skirt and cardigan) that she looked like a cupcake!

funfact:
Ariana is known for her impersonations.

FIRSTS

CONCERT ATTENDED
Katy Perry in the summer of 2011

CELEB CRUSH
Justin Timberlake

FAVE BOY BAND
*NSYNC

COMMUNITY THEATER
WHERE SHE PERFORMED
Little Palm Theatre
for Young People

SONG PERFORMED ONSTAGE
"Somewhere Over the Rainbow" from
The Wizard of Oz

MUSICAL ROLE
The lead role in *Annie* at a
South Florida community theater

BROADWAY PLAY
13

BEAUTY PRODUCT USED
"Lip Smacker's Cotton Candy . . . I
was a little girl, and it tasted good."

Ariana is all smiles when she is surrounded by her fans!

DOING WHAT MAKES HER HAPPY
HOW HIGH WILL THIS SONGBIRD FLY?

"[want to] be doing music for the rest of my life," Ariana told *GL* magazine. "As long as I'm singing, I'm happy."

With the success of her albums, iTunes downloads, and music videos, it looks as if Ariana will be wearing a great big smile for a long time to come. Of course, she has had a lot of new experiences over the past year. "Since 'The Way' came out a lot has happened, a lot has changed," she told *Elle*. "I've been followed around by people with cameras, which is insane to me. I don't really understand it. I was talking to [my managers] about it and they were like, 'Listen, you just need to do

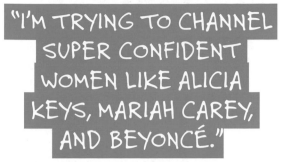

what makes you happy. Don't worry about anything else. Don't get upset. You signed up for this; you're an artist, you're an actress.' I'm not too comfortable with the whole celebrity thing, but I think I'm doing well with the music thing, and that's what makes me happy."

But what road will Ariana take in the future? Music? Acting? Both? She seems pretty sure which way she's headed—going for the high note! She told *Seventeen* magazine, "After *Sam & Cat*, I don't see myself doing much acting. I want to make music that makes people happy. And I just want to enjoy my life. I look back at my old self and think, Ahhh, I've learned so much. I used to struggle for approval. I believed that what other people thought of me was who I am. Every day, I feel like I'm a step closer to being who I'm supposed to be for the rest of my life."

Resources

ARTICLES

Elle.com
"Life Is Grande: Ariana Grande on her Debut Album and the Thrill of Hearing Herself on the Radio"
www.elle.com/news/culture/ariana-grande-interview

Glamour.com
"We Sent Two of Ariana Grande's Biggest Fans to Interview Her—Come See What Happened!"
www.glamour.com/entertainment/blogs/obsessed/2013/09/we-sent-two-of-ariana-grandes.html

Popstar.com
"Exclusive Interview: Ariana Grande"
www.popstar.com/News/Celebrity/Article/909

Facts for Now

Visit this Scholastic Web site for more information on **Ariana Grande**:
www.factsfornow.scholastic.com
Enter the keywords **Ariana Grande**

Glossary

engineered (*en-juh-NEERD*) operated equipment during a recording session

headlining (*HED-ly-ning*) performing as the main act at a concert

karaoke (*kar-ee-OH-kee*) a form of entertainment that originated in Japan in which people sing the words of popular songs to recorded background music

octave (*AHK-tiv*) the eight-note difference on a musical scale between two notes with the same name

stereotypical (*ster-ee-oh-TIP-uh-kuhl*) fitting a widely held but overly simple image of a person, group, or thing

Index

Acknowledgments

Page 6: *First song:* J-14, July 2012
Page 8: *Performing and community theater:* Scholastic, April 27, 2010; *Blurb:* Teen Now, November 2013
Page 9: *Blurb:* Miami Herald, June 12, 2013; *Gloria Estefan meeting:* crushable.com, April 25, 2009
Page 10: *First role, Annie:* wzratv.com
Page 11: *Ariana's family:* Complex.com, November 5, 2013; *Parents' divorce:* Twist February, 2013; *Blurb:* Teen Now, November 2013
Page 12: *Middle school to Broadway:* neonlimelight.com
Page 13: *Blurb:* Complex.com, November 5, 2013
Page 14: *Miami Fans:* Miami Herald, June 17, 2013; *Blurb:* Complex.com, November 5, 2013
Page 16: *Blurb:* Seventeen, August 2013

Page 17: *Broadway/TV:* crushable.com, April 25, 2009; *Blurb:* Twist, March 2013
Page 19: *Blurb:* Teen Now, December 2013
Page 21: *Katy Perry:* Just Jared Jr., August 3, 2012; *Studio:* Elle.com August 22, 2013; *Blurb:* Glamour.com, September 2013
Page 22: *Blurb:* Glamour.com, September 2013; *Mac Miller:* Yahoo.com, September 12, 2013
Page 23: *Music's reach:* Billboard, August 24, 2013
Page 24: *Vocal training:* MTV News, July 20, 2013
Page 25: *Actress/singer:* MTV News; *Blurb:* Elle.com, August 22, 1013
Page 26: *Voice problem:* Twitter, September 12, 2013
Page 27: *New CD:* Yahoo.com, September 12, 2013; *Blurb:* GL, August/September 2013
Page 29: *Dream house:* Teen Now, November 2013

Page 30: *Food:* Twist, September 2013; *Acting advice:* FirstNews.co.uk October 17, 2011; *Singing/acting:* People, November 4, 2013
Page 31: *Red velvet hair:* myjellybean.com; *Perfect day:* Missoandfriends.com
Page 32: *Cat/Ariana:* Seventeen.com
Page 33: *Songwriting:* Scholastic, April 27, 2010; *Favorite books:* Scholastic, April 27, 2010
Page 34: *Broadway in South Africa charity:* Scholastic, April 27, 2010; *First day of school:* Scholastic, April 27, 2010
Page 35: *The Beatles:* Scholastic, April 27, 2010
Page 37: *Most embarrassing moment:* Twist, March 2, 2013

Page 38: *Mac Miller:* MTV News, April 30, 2013; *Kelly Clarkson:* entertainmentwise.com,September 8, 2013; *Demi Lovato:* Billboard May 13, 2013
Page 39: *Avan Jogia:* Just Jared Jr., December 12, 2013; *Scooter Braun:* MTV News, July 1, 2013; *Elizabeth Gillies:* crushable.com, March 14, 2013
Page 40: *Imogen Heap; Judy Garland; India. Arie; Whitney Houston; Brandy:* Billboard,October, 2013
Page 41: *Health advice:* shape.com, February 29, 2012
Page 42: *Personal style; Style advice:* TeenVogue.com
Page 43: *Lip Smacker's:* Seventeen, August 2013
Page 44: *Singing:* GL, August/September 2013; *Change:* Elle.com, August 22, 2013
Page 45: *After Sam & Cat:* Seventeen, August 2013; *Blurbs:* Seventeen, August 2013

About the Author

Marie Morreale is the author of many official and unofficial celebrity biographies. She attended New York University as an English/creative writing major and began her writing and editorial career in New York City. As the editor of teen/music magazines *Teen Machine* and *Jam!*, she covered TV, film, and music personalities and interviewed superstars such as Michael Jackson, Britney Spears, and Justin Timberlake/*NSYNC. Morreale was also an editor/writer at Little Golden Books.

Today, she is the executive editor, Media, of Scholastic Classroom Magazines writing about pop-culture, sports, news, and special events. Morreale lives in New York City and is entertained daily by her two Maine coon cats, Cher and Sullivan.